T

By United Library

https://campsite.bio/unitedlibrary

Table of Contents

Disclaimer

This biography book is a work of nonfiction based on the public life of a famous person. The author has used publicly available information to create this work. While the author has thoroughly researched the subject and attempted to depict it accurately, it is not meant to be an exhaustive study of the subject. The views expressed in this book are those of the author alone and do not necessarily reflect those of any organization associated with the subject. This book should not be taken as an endorsement, legal advice, or any other form of professional advice. This book was written for entertainment purposes only.

Introduction

Taylor Swift's readers are invited to embark on an intimate journey through the remarkable life and career of one of the most influential figures in contemporary music. Taylor Alison Swift, born on December 13, 1989, has not only redefined the boundaries of songwriting but has also left an indelible mark on the music industry and popular culture as a whole.

This meticulously researched biography traces Swift's extraordinary path, from her early beginnings as a 14-year-old aspiring songwriter to becoming a global superstar and cultural icon. Swift's ability to connect with audiences through her lyrics, musical versatility, and artistic reinventions is explored in depth, showcasing her as a prominent cultural figure of the 21st century.

The book delves into Swift's evolution as an artist, starting with her country music roots under the Big Machine Records label and her journey through various musical genres. From country to country pop, rock influences, electronic experimentation, synth-pop, and even hip-hop, Swift's evolution is a testament to her fearless creativity.

Readers gain insight into Swift's chart-topping albums and iconic songs, from "Love Story" to "Shake It Off," "Blank Space," and "Cardigan," each marking a pivotal moment in her career. The book also explores her personal and professional growth, her commitment to artists' rights and women's empowerment, and her record-breaking achievements, including 12 Grammy Awards.

This book is a tribute to an artist whose storytelling prowess has touched the hearts of millions around the world. It's a journey through the life and legacy of a songwriting sensation who continues to inspire and influence generations with her authentic voice and unwavering dedication to her craft.

Taylor Swift

Taylor Alison Swift, born December 13, 1989 in Reading, Pennsylvania, is an American singer-songwriter and actress. Her narrative lyricism, which often draws on her personal experiences, is widely acclaimed by critics and media coverage.

The release of her debut album *Taylor Swift* (2006) made her a country music star. Her song *Tim McGraw* marked her first top 40 hit at the age of sixteen. With *Our Song*, she quickly became the youngest artist to have a single - which she wrote and composed herself - top the music charts. Her second album, *Fearless, was* released in 2008. Supported by two pop singles, *Love Story* and *You Belong with Me*, *Fearless* became the best-selling album in the United States in 2009, and the artist launched her first world tour, the *Fearless Tour*. The album won four Grammy Awards, including "Album of the Year", making Taylor Swift the youngest artist ever to win this award. Her third album, *Speak Now* (2010), sells over a million copies in its first week. Shortly afterwards, Swift embarked on a world tour of over a hundred concerts.

In 2012, she released her fourth album, entitled *Red,* which sold 1.2 million copies in its first week of release and moved away from country sounds to appeal to a broad, international audience. The album's first single, *We Are Never Ever Getting Back Together,* is her first hit to top the *Billboard* Hot 100. The singles that followed were equally successful, including *I Knew You Were Trouble* and *22*.

In 2014, his fifth album *1989* topped the sales charts in 78 countries and, after breaking the pre-order record, sold over 600,000 copies in 24 hours in the United States. In one week, the album sold almost 1.3 million copies, breaking *Red*'s record and becoming the best-selling album in a single week since June 2002 and Eminem's album, *The Eminem Show*. *1989* also marked the singer's consecration as a true international pop star, with one hit after another. It was one of the most awarded pop albums in history, winning the prestigious Grammy for Album of the Year. On the singles front, she became the first female artist to replace herself at the top of the *Billboard Hot 100* with *Blank Space*, dethroning *Shake It Off*.

Her sixth album, *Reputation*, marks a turning point in her career. It is a response to the cyber-harassment she suffered in 2016. In its first week, it sold 1,216,000 copies in the United States. This makes Taylor Swift the only artist in history to consecutively sell four albums in excess of one million copies, the week of their release, in her country. The first single, *Look What You Made Me Do*, appears after long months of media silence from Taylor Swift. Its video, released on August 28, 2017, broke the record for the most-viewed video in one day on YouTube, with 48 million views in 24 hours, and is considered one of the most talked-about comebacks in the music industry.

Taylor Swift returns in 2019 with *Me!*, whose video is viewed over 57 million times in 24 hours. The song is the first single from her seventh album, *Lover*, which also tops the US charts. It also helped her become the most awarded artist in the history of the American Music Awards, beating Michael Jackson's record, in 2019, when she was named Artist of the Decade. She is also named Woman of the Decade by Billboard magazine. After releasing two folk-style albums in 2020, *Folklore* and *Evermore*, once again proving her songwriting skills and widely acclaimed by the international press, Taylor Swift began re-recording her first albums in 2021 to reclaim the rights. She began with *Fearless* and *Red* in 2021, followed by *Speak Now* and *1989* in 2023.

In October 2022, she released her tenth album, *Midnights,* which became the most streamed album in one day on Spotify. On the day of the album's release, Taylor Swift becomes the most streamed music artist in one day on Spotify with 228 million listens in 24 hours, surpassing Bad Bunny. Taylor Swift is the first artist in history to reach the top ten of Billboard's Hot 100. The album reaches number 1 in France in its first week of release, with almost 20,000 sales; this is the first time Taylor Swift has achieved a number 1 in France. The album breaks several records, and marks her comeback in the pop world.

Accumulating nearly 500 awards in just a few years (including eleven Grammy Awards and thirty-two American Music Awards), she has sold over fifty million albums, including thirty-seven million albums in the USA in 2019, making her one of the best-selling artists in history' . *Forbes* magazine named Swift the "highest-paid celebrity of the year" in 2016 and 2019, thanks in part to the Reputation Stadium Tour, the most lucrative tour in U.S. history. In May 2015, she became the youngest person to enter *Forbes'* list of the world's most powerful women. In total, she holds over 35 absolute records in the music world, making her the most powerful artist today. In the USA, journalists and experts refer to her as "The Music Industry" to show just how primary a role she plays in the music industry.

In addition to her musical career, Taylor Swift has appeared in episodes of TV series: she played Haley Jones in *CSI* (2009) and Elaine in *New Girl* (2013), and has had roles in several films: Felicia in the romantic comedy *Valentine's Day* (2010), Audrey in *The Lorax* (2012),

Rosemary in *The Ferryman* (2014), Bombalurina in *Cats* (2019) as well as the role of Elizabeth Meekins in *Amsterdam* (2022).

Biography

Youth (1989-2004)

Taylor Swift was born on December 13, 1989 in Reading, Pennsylvania. Her father, Scott Kingsley Swift (born March 5, 1952), is a financial advisor with Merrill Lynch' . His mother, Andrea Gardner Swift (née Finlay, January 10, 1958), is a homemaker and previously worked as a mutual fund marketing manager. Andrea Swift spent the first ten years of her life in Singapore, where her Pennsylvania-born father was an engineer and heir to three generations of bank presidents, before moving to Texas. On February 20, 1988, Andrea Swift married Scott Swift in Harris County. Swift takes her first name from the American singer James Taylor; her mother thought a neutral name would help her forge a successful career. She has a younger brother, Austin Kingsley Swift (born March 11, 1992), who graduated from the University of Notre-Dame-du-Lac.

Taylor Swift grew up in a devout, practicing Christian family of the Catholic faith" . In her youth, she attended church services every Sunday, and took part in spiritual retreats to study the Bible in rural Pennsylvania. She sang weekly in the church choir with her grandmother, Marjorie Finlay, a former classical opera singer. Swift recalls those moments shared together in church: "I remember [my grandmother] singing, the thrill of it. She was one of my first inspirations."

Taylor Swift was pre-schooled at the private Catholic Alvernia Montessori School run by the Franciscan Sisters, where she developed an early interest in music and singing . The school's head teacher, Sister Ann Marie Coll, recalls: "She was a little shy, but not too shy, and always liked to sing. Taylor wasn't stubborn, but she was a determined little girl. When she focused on something, she was very determined. She went on to attend the private Wyndcroft School. At the age of nine, Swift moved with her family to Wyomissing, where she attended West Reading Elementary Center and Wyomissing Area Junior/Senior High School.

Swift spent part of her childhood on an eleven-hectare Christmas tree farm in Montgomery County, Pennsylvania. She spends her summer vacations at her family's home in Stone Harbor, New Jersey, and describes the place as "where most of her childhood memories were made." One of Swift's earliest passions was classical riding, her mother having put her in the saddle at nine months; thereafter, Swift competed in horse shows. Her parents owned several Quarter Horses and a Shetland pony. In fourth grade, she won a national poetry contest with her poem *A Monster In My Closet.*

At the age of nine, Swift began to take an interest in musicals, appearing in productions such as *Grease*, *Annie*, *Bye Bye Birdie* and *The Sound of Music* [insufficient source]. She regularly traveled to Broadway to take singing and acting lessons. However, after spending several years auditioning in New York and getting nowhere, Swift became interested in country music. She spent her weekends singing at local festivals, fairs, cafés, karaoke contests, clubs and hospitals. At the age of eleven, after several attempts, Swift won a local talent show competition after singing LeAnn Rimes' *Big Deal*, and had the opportunity to perform at a Charlie Daniels concert at an amphitheater in Strausstown, Pennsylvania. Her ambition and interest in country music began to separate Swift from her classmates.

After watching an episode of *Behind the Music* (a documentary program in which each episode focuses on a popular musician or band) with Faith Hill, Swift wanted to move to Nashville, Tennessee, for her musical career. She went there with her mother during her spring break to offer recordings of herself singing Dolly Parton and Dixie Chicks songs to Music Row labels, in the hope of being signed by one of them. She was repeatedly rejected, and realized that "everyone in this town wanted to do what I wanted to do. So I kept telling myself that I had to find a way to stand out. At the age of eleven, she sang the American national anthem at a Philadelphia Sixers game in front of a crowd of 20,000, a dream she realized without a record label. When Swift was twelve, a computer repairman taught her to play guitar, and she used the three chords he taught her to write her first song, *Lucky You*. In 2003, Swift and her parents teamed up with a New York manager, Dan Dymtrow, with whose help Swift became a model for Abercrombie & Fitch's Rising Stars campaign and met several record labels. After singing at a concert organized by RCA Records, she travels back and forth between Wyomissing and Nashville.

At the age of fourteen, his father left Pennsylvania's Merrill Lynch bank for Nashville's, and the family moved to a lake house in Hendersonville, Tennessee. Swift later describes this as an incredible sacrifice made by her family: "My parents saw that this was really an obsession, that I wasn't going to let it go and that it wasn't a teenage whim. They were thrown into it [...] We had no idea what we were doing. My parents bought me a book on the music industry." In Tennessee, Swift attended Hendersonville High School for her first and second years. For her third and fourth years, she attended Aaron Academy, a private Christian school offering home tuition. In 2008, she graduated .

Debut and *Taylor Swift* (2004-2006)

As part of her artistic development with RCA Records, Swift participates in songwriting sessions alongside experienced songwriters such as Troy Verges, Brett Beavers, Brett James, Mac McAnally and The Warren Brothers' . She eventually formed a lasting relationship with Liz Rose, whom she assisted at a songwriters' event, and with whom she wrote several songs. They met every Tuesday after school for songwriting sessions. Rose explains that these sessions with Swift were "the easiest I've ever done. Basically, I was just her editor. She would write about what had happened to her at school that day. She had a very clear vision of what she was trying to say. And she'd come up with incredible hooks." She also recorded a few demos with producer Nathan Chapman.

After performing at a showcase for BMI in New York, Swift became the youngest artist ever hired by the music publishing house, Sony/ATV Music Publishing. At the age of fifteen, she left RCA Records; the label wanted to wait until she came of age (21) to release her first album, so she felt ready to launch her own career' . She also parted company with her manager Dan Dymtrow, who subsequently filed a lawsuit against her and her parents. "I really felt I was running out of time." Swift later declares, "I wanted to take the opportunity to record what I was going through in an album." During a showcase at the Blue Bird café in 2005, Swift caught the attention of Scott Borchetta (en), an executive producer at DreamWorks Records who was about to set up his own label, Big Machine Records. She became one of his first artists, and her father received a 3% stake in the young company. For her first time in the country music world, Scott Borchetta arranges for Swift to perform at the CMA Music Festival (en).

Swift launched her self-titled debut album shortly afterwards. Having written alongside experienced songwriters, Swift convinced Big Machine Records to take the demo she had recorded for producer Nathan Chapman (en). It was Scott Borchetta's first studio recording, but Swift felt they had the right "feel." Eventually, Chapman produced all but one of the songs on her debut album. She describes the album as her "diary", revealing all her youth. She declares, "even though I look like I've had 500 boyfriends," many of the songs are observational. Swift wrote three songs herself, including two singles, and co-wrote the rest of the album alongside songwriters such as Liz Rose, Robert Ellis Orralln and Angelo Petraglia. Musically, the *Taylor Swift* album released in October 2006, is described as "a mix between traditional country and rock guitars." *PopMatters* states that it hopes Swift "will be able to find a compromise between traditional country and her obvious pop sensibilities, because *Taylor Swift* suggests she can do better." The *New Yorker*'s Sasha Frere-Jones describes Swift as a "prodigy". He also compliments the lyrics of the single *Our Song*: "He had one hand on the wheel, the other on my heart." *Country Weekly* felt that "the most thoughtful material suggests a talent ready to last well beyond high school." *Rolling Stone* describes Swift as "bright-eyed but remarkably experienced" and admires *Our Song* for its lilting melody reminiscent of Britney Spears and Patsy Cline.

Singles and promotional tour (2007-2008)

Big Machine Records was still in its infancy when Swift released her first single, *Tim McGraw,* in June 2006. With the help of her mother, Swift sent demos of the single to several radio stations. She spent 2006 promoting *Taylor Swift* with a radio tour, commenting later: "Radio tours, for most artists, last six weeks. As far as I'm concerned, mine lasted six months". Swift baked cookies and painted canvases for everyone involved in her tour. She appeared on TV shows such as *Grand Ole Opry*, *Good Morning America* and *Total Request Live*. She has also signed on as spokesperson for the L.e.i. clothing brand⸍ . Swift describes herself as "a child of the Internet", using

Myspace to build up a fan base. She wrote her own messages, left comments on her fans' accounts and replied personally to her fans. During this period, it was "revolutionary in country music." Scott Borchetta says his decision to sign a 16-year-old singer-songwriter initially shocked his acquaintances in the music industry, but Swift was tapping into a previously unknown market: teenage girls who listen to country music. Following the release of *Tim McGraw*, four more singles were released between 2007 and 2008: *Teardrops on My Guitar*, *Our Song*, *Picture to Burn* and *Should've Said No*. They all scored hits on the Hot Country Songs chart, with *Our Song* and *Should've Said No* topping the charts. *Our Song* made Swift the youngest artist ever to have a self-penned single top the charts, and *Teardrops on My Guitar was* a minor success compared with the other singles, reaching number thirteen on the Billboard Hot 100. The album sold over 39,000 copies in its first week; by March 2011, it had sold over 5.5 million copies worldwide. In October 2007, she released a Christmas album entitled *Sounds of the Season: The Taylor Swift Holiday Collection*, as well as an EP, *Beautiful Eyes*, released in July 2008ʹ .

Swift tours extensively to promote her album. In addition to festival and theater dates, she opened for numerous country music artists. In late 2006, she opened for Rascal Flatts on the last date of their Me & My Gang Tour, after the previous opening act, Eric Church, was fired. In 2007, she opened for George Strait on twenty dates, Kenny Chesney on several dates, Brad Paisley on a few dates and Faith Hill and her husband Tim McGraw on several dates. In 2008, she returned to the road with the band Rascal Flatts for their Still Feels Good Tour. As well as performing her own songs, Swift does a number of covers of Beyoncé, Rihanna, John Waite, Lynyrd Skynyrd and Eminem". She holds several four-hour meet-and-greet sessions with fans after her concerts. In 2007, Swift and Alan Jackson were named "Artist of the Year" at the Nashville Songwriters Association International; she was the youngest artist ever to hold this title. She was also honored in the "Best New Artist" category at the Country Music Association Awards. In 2008, she was named "New Female Artist" at the Academy of Country Music Awards, and "Favorite Female Country Artist" at the American Music Awards. She received seven BMI Awards for singles from her album *Taylor Swift*. She is also nominated at the 2008 Grammy Awards for "Best New Artist", but Amy Winehouse wins.

Fearless and collaborations (2008-2009)

In November 2008, Swift released her second album, *Fearless*. She wrote seven songs herself, including two singles, and co-wrote the other six with Liz Rose (en), John Rich, Colbie Caillat and Hillary Lindsey (en). She also co-produced the album with Nathan Chapman. Musically, the album is described as "noisy with guitars and uncatchy choruses," with "a bit of fiddle and banjo hidden in the mix." *The New York Times* describes Swift as "one of pop music's best songwriters, pragmatic above all else, and more in touch with her intimate life than most adults." *The Village Voice* feels "she exhibited supernatural wisdom and inclusiveness [...] masterfully avoiding the typical pitfalls of the overly banal columnist as well as false depths." *Rolling Stone* notes that despite her "almost impersonal professionalism" based on verse-chorus-bridge automatisms, her songs exude a teenage naiveté that is "very intimate and authentic". *USA Today* finds it "pleasing to hear a talented young adult in teenage guise." *The New Yorker* describes the album as "without false notes", adding that the best being *Fifteen* "will remain in people's minds for years to come." *Entertainment Weekly* notes, however, that it would appeal most to young girls - "she gives the impression of being a real teenager and not a pestering, manufactured Lolita" - but also declares that it would be "exciting to see her precocious talent evolve." Music critic Robert Christgau describes Swift as "a rare and impossible force and a very talented teenager."

Swift then organizes a huge promotional tour for *Fearless*. An episode of *The Ellen DeGeneres Show* is dedicated to the album launch, and Swift appears on several talk shows. She communicates with fans via Twitter and

Skype. She launches a line of summer dresses with L.e.i. for Walmart, greeting cards, and dolls' . She also becomes a spokesperson for the Nashville Predators and Sony Cyber-shot, and takes part in advertising for the *Band Hero* video game. Swift pays tribute to numerous artists during her television appearances: Alan Jackson's *Drive (For Daddy Gene)* for the CMT Giants event, George Strait's *Run*, and she takes part in Def Leppard's televised concert in Nashville. In 2009, she performs her song *Fifteen* alongside Miley Cyrus at the Grammy Awards, raps alongside T-Pain at the CMT Awards, then presents *Saturday Night Live*. The album's first single, *Love Story,* is released in September 2008, becoming the second best-selling single of all time, and reaching number 4 on the *Billboard Hot 100*. Between 2008 and 2009, she releases four singles: *White Horse*, *You Belong with Me*, *Fifteen* and *Fearless*. *You Belong with Me* is the best-selling single, reaching number two on the *Billboard Hot 100*. The album reaches #1 on the *Billboard 200* after selling over 592,304 copies in its first week of release. *Fearless* remained at the top of the *Billboard 200* for a total of 11 non-consecutive weeks, and since then has sold over 8.6 million copies worldwide in 2008, making it the best-selling album of 2009.

Swift embarked on her first headline tour between April 2009 and June 2010. Her 105-date Fearless Tour includes 90 dates in North America, 6 in Europe, 8 in Australia, and one in Asia. The elaborate staging includes a fairytale castle and a high-school bandstand; she also covers Justin Timberlake's *What Goes Around... Comes Around*, mixing it with Justin Timberlake's *You're Not Sorry*. During her North American tour, she is joined by Katy Perry, Faith Hill and John Mayer" . Justin Bieber, Kellie Pickler and Gloriana opened for her. In all, the tour attracts over 1.1 million fans and grosses $63 million. A documentary on her tour, *Journey to Fearless, is* broadcast on American television and released on Blu-Ray. Meanwhile, she opened for Keith Urban on his Escape Together World Tour. In June 2009, she recorded a new version of Tom Petty's *American Girl* and continued to make her mark on the scene with this cover.

Fearless wins several awards and becomes the most awarded album in the history of country music. Swift becomes the youngest artist ever, and one of six women named "Artist of the Year" by the Country Music Association. *Fearless* also wins the "Album of the Year" award. The American Music Awards honor Swift in the "Artist of the Year" and "Favorite Country Album" categories. She also wins four BMI Awards. *Billboard* names her "Artist of the Year 2009." She also makes the "100 Most Influential People" list in 2010.

She took part in John Mayer's fourth album, singing backing vocals on his single *Half of My Heart* in November

2009. John Mayer wrote the song as a tribute to Tom Petty and Fleetwood Mac: "I thought: Well, if this was going to be my love letter to this kind of music, who would be the Stevie Nicks in this equation? And I thought: This Taylor Swift is going to be around for a long time." Between 2008 and 2009, Swift collaborated with a number of artists. She co-wrote a single for Kellie Pickler, *Best Days of Your Life* (2008), on which she sang backing vocals. She co-wrote two songs for the film *Hannah Montana, the movie* (2009) - *You'll Always Find Your Way Back Home* and *Crazier* - with Martin Johnson and Robert Ellis Orrall (en). She also sings a duet with the group Boys Like Girls entitled *Two Is Better Than One* (2009), written by Martin Johnson. In January 2010, she recorded two songs: *Today Was a Fairytale* for the soundtrack of the film *Valentine's Day* and a cover of Better Than Ezra's *Breathless* for the album *Hope for Haiti Now*.

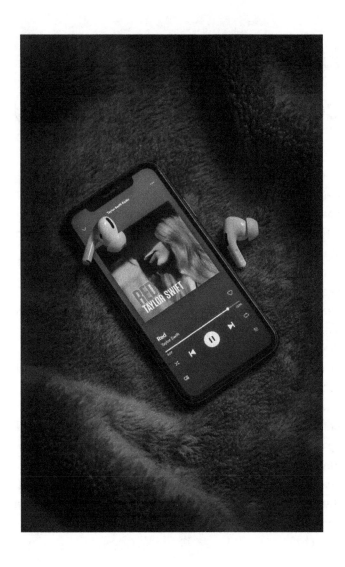

MTV Awards and VMA controversy (2009-2010)

In September 2009, Swift became the first country artist to win an MTV Video Music Award when her single *You Belong with Me was* nominated for "Best Video of the Year by a Female Artist." Her acceptance speech is interrupted by rapper Kanye West, who has already been involved in several scandals during awards ceremonies. Kanye West declares that Beyoncé deserved to win this year's MTV Video Music Awards for "Best Video of the Year by a Female Artist" because, in his opinion, her video *Single Ladies (Put a Ring on It)* is "the best video of all time." The crowd booed Kanye West, prompting him to give them the finger. He then hands the microphone back to Swift, who is speechless. Backstage, Swift is seen in tears. According to *Rolling Stone*, during a confrontation between Swift's mother and Kanye West, the latter "paid lip service to his apology and added that he still thought Beyoncé's video deserved to win." Kanye was therefore dismissed from the ceremony. Later, when Beyoncé won the MTV Video Music Awards for "Video of the Year", she invited Swift to join her on stage to finish her acceptance speech.

In the press room at the ceremony, Swift was asked by reporters if she had any "grudges" against Kanye West: "I don't know him and I've never met him, so.... I don't want to start anything because tonight I'm having a good time'." The evening's incident attracts media attention and inspires many Internet memes. President Barack Obama himself calls Kanye West a "moron", and former President Jimmy Carter declares that Kanye's interruption was "totally inappropriate." His behavior is subsequently criticized by celebrities such as Eminem, Snoop Dogg and Madonna'. Kanye apologized for his verbal outburst on two blogs and even during his appearance on The *Jay Leno Show'*. He does, however, stand by what he said that night, saying that while he thinks Swift is "very talented, Beyoncé's video was the best of this decade. I gave my award to OutKast because he deserved it more than I did... I'm not crazy, I'm just realistic." Two days later, Swift claimed that Kanye hadn't spoken to her since the incident. Kanye then contacted her to offer to apologize in person, which Swift accepted: "Kanye called me and he was really sincere when he apologized to me". She refuses to discuss the incident in interviews so that it doesn't become a "bigger issue": "It happened on TV, so everyone saw what happened.... I don't feel the need to keep talking about it." It is said that the incident and the media attention around it makes Swift "a bona fide celebrity."

In January 2010, Swift won four Grammy Awards out of a total of eight nominations. *Fearless* was named "Album of the Year" and "Best Country Album", while *White Horse* was named "Best Country Song" and "Best Performance by a Female Country Artist." During the ceremony, she performs Stevie Nicks' *Rhiannon* and *You Belong with Me* with Stevie Nicks. But both her performances were negatively received, prompting widespread media reaction'. Her voice is described as "heavily fake", "astonishingly bad" and "incredibly pitiful'." While *The New York Times* finds it "interesting to see someone so talented commit the occasional blunder" and describes Swift as "the most important new pop star in recent years," music industry personality Bob Lefsetz predicts that her career will end overnight. He publicly appeals to Swift's father to hire a "crisis publicist" to handle the story, as "Taylor is too young and stupid to understand the mistake she just made'." In April 2010, Stevie Nicks defended Swift, saying, "Taylor reminds me of myself with her determination and childishness. It's a naiveté that's so special and so rare. This girl writes songs that make everyone sing, like Neil Diamond or Elton John... The female rock-'n'-roll-country-pop artist has returned, and her name is Taylor Swift. And it's women like her who are going to save the music industry.

Following the incident at the 2009 MTV Awards, Kanye West used his Twitter account in September 2010 to apologize to Swift, referring to her as "a little girl with dreams like the rest of us": "I wrote a song for Taylor Swift, it's so beautiful and I want her to have it. If she turns it down, then I'll sing it for her." Later, at the 2010 MTV Video Music Awards, Swift performed the song *Innocent*, addressed to Kanye West and described by *The Washington Post* as "a little masterpiece of passive aggression, a vivisection disguised as a peace offering." Music critics find his performance too serious and "mean-spirited". In October 2010, Kanye West declared that it was a "mistake" to have named the album *Fearless* Best Album of the Year at the Grammy Awards. In November 2010, Kanye declared that he didn't see how his interruption at the 2009 VMAs was "so arrogant" and described his actions as "selfless". He also adds that it was "disrespectful" and "retarded" for Swift to have been nominated in the same category as Beyoncé. He claims that thanks to his intervention, Swift "made the front page of a hundred magazines and sold over a million albums in one week." He also claims that "if I hadn't been drunk, I could have stayed on stage longer... Taylor never came to my defense in any interview. And she rode the waves, she rode and rode ...." At the Costume Institute Gala in May 2011, Swift and Kanye came face to face on the red carpet; they shook hands.

Speak Now (2010-2011)

Swift released her third album, *Speak Now,* in October 2010. She wrote all twelve songs on the album herself. Swift, who co-produced the album with Nathan Chapman, describes it as "a collection of confessions - things I wish I'd said at a particular time." Initially, she wanted to call the album *Enchanted*, but Scott Borchetta told her that this title didn't reflect the album's more adult themes.

Musically, the album is said to "extend beyond country-pop to border both alternative rock and bubblegum pop." *USA Today* declares that Swift's songwriting skills would remind listeners "what all the fuss was about in the first place" and that the album grabs hold of "the sweet pain of becoming an adult." *Los Angeles Times is full of* praise for her songwriting ability, as "she's able to talk about common experiences but make them unique." *The New York Times* describes the album as "wild, musically varied, excellent and probably the best." *The Village Voice* finds that the album demanded "a real appreciation of Taylor's talent, which is not confessional but dramatic: like a procession of country songwriters before her, Taylor creates characters and situations - drawn from real life - and finds powerful ways to describe them." *Entertainment Weekly* notes that love may confound her, but "the art of the Songcraft expert does not." Music critic, John Christgau (en), finds the songs on the album "too long and overworked" but notes "they show an effort to bring out the broadest and best emotions."

Rolling Stone describes Swift as "one of the best songwriters in country, pop or rock": "Taylor may be a slick Nashville pro who knows all the tricks to make a song a hit, but she's also very nervous, a hyper-romantic girl with a melodramatic streak the size of the Atchafalaya River."

Prior to the release of *Speak Now*, Swift embarked on an extensive promotional campaign. She appeared on several TV shows and gave several free mini-concerts in unusual locations, including Hollywood Boulevard and a waiting room at John F. Kennedy International Airport. She took part in a "guitar raffle" with Kris Kristofferson, Emmylou Harris, Vince Gill and Lionel Richie at Club Nokia in Los Angeles; the musicians shared the stage and took turns singing acoustic versions of their songs to raise money for the Country Music Hall of Fame. She later became a spokesperson for the CoverGirl (en) brand. She also launched her own fragrance, *Wonderstruck,* in collaboration with Elizabeth Arden, followed by a special edition of *Speak Now* with Target Corporation. In August 2010, she released the first single from the *Speak Now* album, *Mine,* and five further singles were released between 2010 and 2011: *Back to December*, *Mean*, *The Story of Us*, *Sparks Fly*, and *Ours*. *Speak Now was* a major commercial success, topping the *Billboard 200* and selling over 1,047,000 copies, making it the sixteenth album in U.S. history to sell over a million copies in just one week.

By February 2012, the album had sold 5.7 million copies worldwide.

Speak Now World Tour and Grammy Awards (2011-2012)

Throughout 2011 and into early 2012, Swift embarked on the Speak Now World Tour. In thirteen months, she performed 111 dates, including seven in Asia, twelve in Europe, eighty in North America and twelve in Australia. The staging was inspired by a Broadway musical, with choreography and costumes' . Swift also invited a number of celebrities on his North American tour: James Vernon Swift, Jason Mraz, Shawn Colvin, Johnny Rzeznik, Andy Grammer, Tal Bachman, Selena Gomez, Justin Bieber, Nicki Minaj, Nelly, B.o.B, Usher, Flo Rida, T.I., Jon Foreman, Jim Adkins, Hayley Williams, Hot Chelle Rae, Ronnie Dunn, Darius Rucker, Tim McGraw and Kenny Chesney' . During her U.S. tour, Swift wrote a different phrase on her left arm for each concert, later declaring that it represented her state of mind. She also played a number of acoustic covers, then paid tribute to an artist born in each of the cities she visited. She says acoustic covers allow her to be more "spontaneous". The tour attracts over 1.6 million fans and grosses over $123 million. Swift releases her first Live album, *Speak Now World Tour: Live* on November 21, 2011. In July 2012, James Taylor invites Swift to Tanglewood; they play the songs *Fire and Rain, Love Story* and *Ours* together. James Taylor, who met Swift at the age of 18, declares that "we hit it off. I really like his songs, and his stage presence was great'."

At the Grammy Awards in February 2012, the single *Mean* was selected in the "Best Country Song" and "Best Solo Performance" categories. Music critic Bob Lefsetz, who had criticized her negatively for her performance at the 2010 Grammy Awards, thought the song was dedicated to him. Bob Lefsetz had previously encouraged Swift in her career, and they spoke frequently by phone or message. *Time* feels that she "made a comeback by singing right, and that she had revenge to exact", and *USA Today* notes that all the bad reviews that were said in 2010 "transformed her into a better songwriter as well as a better performer." In March 2012, she took part in the soundtrack for the film *Hunger Games*. She co-wrote and performed the song *Safe and Sound* as a duet with The Civil Wars and T-Bone Burnett. John Paul White declares that working with Swift was "a revelation. She had great ideas. We were really free. It was really a collaboration. We brought melancholy and a darker angle. Taylor brought the melody and the chords." *Rolling Stone* describes the song as "her most beautiful ballad." In January 2012, Swift and The Civil Wars composed a live version of the song at Nashville's Ryman Auditorium. *Safe and Sound was* then released and billed as the first single from the film's soundtrack, and by July 2012 had sold over a million copies in the US. She then recorded another song for the film's soundtrack entitled *Eyes Open*, written and produced by Nathan Chapman. In May 2012, she recorded a duet with rapper B.o.B entitled *Both of Us* for the latter's second album, *Strange Clouds*.

Red (2012-2013)

In October 2012, Swift released her fourth album, *Red*. She writes nine songs on her own and co-writes the other seven with: Max Martin, Liz Rose, Dan Wilson, Ed Sheeran and Gary Lightbody. Nathan Chapman is the album's main producer, but so are Jeff Bhasker, Butch Walker, Jacknife Lee, Dann Huff and Shellback. Nathan Chapman says he encouraged Swift "to branch out and imagine herself in other situations." She describes the collaborative process as "an apprenticeship." *Red* examines drama-filled romantic relationships; she later explains that, since writing the album, such relationships no longer appeal to her. Musically, she experiments with heartland rock, dubstep and dance-pop' . *The Guardian* describes Swift as a "Brunehilde of a rockstar" and the album as "another chapter in one of the most beautiful fantasies pop music has ever constructed." Jon Caramanica (en) of *The New York Times* magazine awards *Red* second place on his "Albums of the Year" list stating that, in this album, "Taylor stops pretending she's anything but a pop star, an album with adult concerns for example, how two bodies communicate with each other and how taste in albums can be a stand-in for moral turpitude." However, he also declares that "while often excellent, this album is his most uneven." *The Times is full of* praise for his "sublime lyrics", especially those of the song *All Too Well*. Salon.com claims that "in addition to the Serious Female Singer Songwriters token, Taylor reminds me of the masters of quirky, heartfelt pop like Alex Chilton and Jonathan Richman."

As part of Red's promotional campaign, representatives from 72 radio stations - worldwide - are flown to Nashville the week the album is released to interview Swift. She also appears on several TV shows and plays at numerous awards ceremonies in the U.S., as well as in the U.K., Germany and Australia. She also offers exclusive promotion via Target, Papa John's Pizza and Walgreens. She also becomes the face of shoe brand Keds, releases her second fragrance with Elizabeth Arden, and continues to be the face of CoverGirl, Sony Electronics and American Greetings.

In August 2012, Swift released the first single from *Red* entitled *We Are Never Ever Getting Back Together*, which became her first hit to top the *Billboard Hot 100*, the track downloading 636,000 copies in its first week, not only the biggest digital week for a female artist but also the second biggest in history. Three more singles followed: the internationally successful *I Knew You Were Trouble*, *Begin Again* and *22*. *Red* peaked at #1 on the Billboard 200, selling over 1.21 million copies in its first week, making Swift the first female artist to sell nearly 2 million albums just one week after its release. The album also tops the charts in the UK, Ireland, Canada, Brazil, Argentina, Mexico, Japan, Malaysia, Australia and New Zealand. In November 2012, sales figures are announced at over 2.8 million copies worldwide. Then, in the same month, it is announced that, over the course of her career, Swift sells more than 26 million albums and 75 million downloads of her songs worldwide. In March 2013, Swift begins her world tour, the Red Tour, until September 2013, with 62 concerts scheduled in North America.

Meanwhile, Swift provides backing vocals with Keith Urban on Tim McGraw's *Highway Don't Care*, which will appear on her twelfth studio album *Two Lanes of Freedom,* due for release on February 5, 2013. She is also writing a song with Justin Bieber, the release date of which is still unknown. Justin's manager, Scooter Braun, says the song is being created with a specific project behind it; it could be on Justin's album, *Believe Acoustic*. Swift is nominated three times at the Grammy Awards on February 10, 2013; *We Are Never Ever Getting Back Together* is nominated in the "Single of the Year" category, and *Safe and Sound* in the "Best Country Duo" and "Best Song Written for a Motion Picture." Swift is present at the NRJ Music Awards 2013, this 14^e ceremony of which took place on January 26, 2013 live from Midem in Cannes. She performs her world-famous hit *We Are Never Ever Getting Back Together*. Swift began writing songs for her fifth album in July 2013. On August 14, 2013, Swift wins two awards at the Teen Choice Awards: "Best Female Country Artist" and "Best Country Single". On August 25, 2013, she won the second Video Music Award of her career: for Best Video for a Female Artist with the song *I Knew You Were Trouble*. By September 2013, *Red had* sold over 6 million copies.

Transition to pop and *1989* (2014-2016)

At the end of 2013, Swift declared that she had been working on her fifth album since July 2013, scheduled for release at the end of 2014. In November 2013, she reveals, "There are about seven or eight songs ready that will be on my next album. The project is heading towards a whole new sound and that's all I wanted." Taylor Swift declares in *Miss Americana that it was the* fact that *Red didn*'t win the Grammy for Album of the Year that made her decide to change her style. She also composes more than three songs with producers Max Martin and Shellback. Composers Diane Warren and Ryan Tedder are also working on the new album with the singer, saying: "Taylor writes her own songs.... She's probably the fastest songwriter we've ever met in our lives." Subsequently, Swift expresses her desire to work with Sia Furler, Jack Antonoff and Imogen Heap on her fifth album. In July 2014, Swift declared that the first single, entitled *Shake It Off*, would be released on August 18, with the album to follow on October 27, 2014. The following month, Swift announced that she would exclusively sing the first single from her fifth album at the MTV Video Music Awards on August 24, 2014.

Taylor Swift describes this new opus as her first "official" pop record. In the U.S., *Shake It Off* goes straight to #1 on the *Billboard* Hot 100 and stays there for four non-consecutive weeks, signing the best debut of 2014 with 544,000 downloads; it's also the fourth-best digital week in history. The title is a resounding success around the world, reaching number one in many countries including Canada and Australia. As part of the album's promotion, Swift invites fans to listening sessions, which she calls "1989 secret sessions", during September at her homes in Nashville, New York, Los Angeles and Rhode Island. On October 9, 2014, Swift announced via her Instagram account that a second song from her album, entitled *Out of the Woods*, would be released on October 14, 2014; the track took the top spot on the Hot Digital Songs chart with 195,000 downloads. The following week, on October 20, 2014, she releases the promotional single *Welcome to*

New York; all proceeds from the sale of the single are donated to the New York Department of Education.

The album *1989 is* released on October 27, 2014, and sells over 600,000 copies in 24 hours. Just two days after its release, over 751,000 copies of the album are sold. A week later sales reach 1,287,000 million records; Taylor Swift thus becomes the only artist in history to consecutively sell three albums in excess of one million copies, in the United States, the week of their release' . The album was a commercial and critical success, signing the best debut for a female artist in the UK in 2014 and ranking first in many countries including notably Australia, Belgium, Canada, and Norway" . On November 10, 2014, she released the second official single, *Blank Space*; the track reached number one on the *Billboard* Hot 100 while dethroning *Shake It Off*. Taylor Swift thus becomes the first woman in the 56-year history of the *Billboard* Hot 100 to succeed herself at number one; the track will remain at the top of the Hot 100 for seven non-consecutive weeks and becomes the second-best week of 2014 with 503,000 copies sold during Christmas week. The Blank Space video is one of the most viewed on YouTube today, with over 3 billion views. The track was also nominated for a Grammy for Song of the Year in 2016. In the United States, *1989* sold 3.66 million copies in 2014, becoming the best-selling album of the year. The album also stayed at number one on the *Billboard* 200 for

11 non-consecutive weeks making Taylor Swift the second woman after Whitney Houston (who did it with three albums) to have managed ten weeks at the top of the *Billboard* 200 with two of her albums (*Fearless* being the first). On May 5, 2015, she kicks off her fourth *The 1989* World Tour in Japan, which ends on December 12 in Australia. Vance Joy and Shawn Mendes open the concerts.

In February 2015, Taylor Swift was crowned by the International Federation of the Phonographic Industry (IFPI) as the best-selling artist of 2014. On February 9, 2015, she releases the single *Style*, which reaches number six on the *Billboard* Hot 100. The fourth single, *Bad Blood*, is unveiled at the *Billboard* Music Awards on May 17, 2015, with a different version to the one featured on the album having added rapper Kendrick Lamar and supported by a celebrity-studded video, this one will break the YouTube views record in 24 hours with 20.1 million views. The track also reached number one on the *Billboard* Hot 100 for a week. The fifth single, *Wildest Dreams* follows on August 31, 2015 and reaches number five on the *Billboard* Hot 100, then the sixth single *Out Of The Woods* is unveiled on February 5, 2016 and reaches number eighteen. The same year, she appears on stage, on guitar, accompanying Madonna as she performs *Ghosttown* to promote her album *Rebel Heart*.

On February 15, 2016, at the 58ᵉ Grammy Awards
ceremony, she won Album of the Year for *1989*, becoming
the first female artist in history to win the award twice, as
well as Best Pop Album and Best Music Video for *Bad
Blood*. However, she failed to win Recording of the Year,
Song of the Year and Best Pop Song for *Blank Space*, and
Best Pop Duo for *Bad Blood*.

Back with *Reputation* (2017-2018)

On August 25, 2017, Taylor Swift announced the title and
release date of her next album, *Reputation* (stylized as
"*reputation*"), scheduled for release on November 10 of
the same year.its common thread is the singer's "death of
reputation" and the answers she wants to provide. On
October 26, 2017, Swift released her second single,
...Ready for it? Gorgeous (en) and *Call It What You Want
(en)* follow shortly afterwards.

In the week of its release in the United States, *Reputation*
sold over 1.2 million copies, making it the best-selling
album of 2017. Taylor Swift thus becomes the first singer
to pass the million sales mark four times in a single week.

On January 12, 2018, Taylor Swift unveiled the music
video for *End Game*, the third single from her album
Reputation, featuring British singer Ed Sheeran and
American rapper Future. *End Game* was first performed
on December 2, 2017 at iHeartRadio's Jingle Ball, and

received mixed reviews at the time. Having tried her hand at science fiction with *...Ready For It?*, this time the singer embarks on a colorful and festive world tour, illustrating her nocturnal escapades in Miami, Tokyo and London. Directed by Joseph Kahn, with whom Swift signs her seventh collaboration, the video racked up 2 million views in just a few hours.

The tour she embarks on from May 8, 2018, the *Reputation Stadium Tour*, becomes the most lucrative tour in US history raking in over $266 million.

Lover (2019-2020)

In early 2019, the palette used by Taylor Swift on Instagram changed radically, abandoning the dark shades and snakes of the *Reputation* era for more cheerful pastel hues. This change is interpreted by fans and journalists alike as a sign of the imminent arrival of a new album.

On April 13, Taylor Swift officially launched the promotion of her new album with a 13-day countdown. With 1 day to go, on April 25, she poses next to a butterfly mural in Nashville, Tennessee. On April 26, Taylor Swift made a comeback with her new single *Me!* a duet with Brendon Urie of Panic! at the Disco, which climbed from 100^e to 2^e on the *Billboard* 100 in just one week.

On June 14, Swift releases her second single *You Need to Calm Down*, which also reaches #2 on the *Billboard* Hot

100 and whose video, which denounces homophobia and defends the rights of the LGBT community, wins the MTV VMA for Video of the Year. Taylor Swift announces the release date of her seventh album, *Lover,* on August 23, 2019.

Lover, is a rather well-received album, although it doesn't match its predecessors in terms of sales and awards'. It debuted at number one on the *Billboard* 200, but only stayed there for a week. However, it enabled her to become the most awarded artist in the history of the American Music Awards, beating Michael Jackson's record, in 2019, during which ceremony she was named Artist of the Decade.

During the promotion of *Lover*, she clashes with Scooter Braun over the rights to her early albums, which he owns after buying out her record label. He offered to buy them back on condition of releasing a new album for each old album bought back under a new contract with Big Machine Records, which the singer refused. She began re-recording her old albums in November 2020.

The song *Beautiful Ghosts (en)*, which she co-wrote with Andrew Lloyd Webber for the *Cats* soundtrack, is nominated for a Golden Globe for Best Film Score but does not win the statuette. In 2020, a documentary dedicated to her was released on Netflix: *Miss Americana*.

Change of style with *Folklore* and *Evermore* (2020)

During the Covid-19 pandemic, she unexpectedly released two new albums: *folklore* on July 24 and *evermore* on December 11, 2020′ .

As an indie folk, alternative rock, electro-folk and chamber pop album, *folklore* marks a departure from the upbeat pop sound of Swift's previous studio albums to mellow tunes driven by piano and guitar, with production by Aaron Dessner (en) and Jack Antonoff. Joe Alwyn co-wrote a few songs under the pseudonym William Bowery. The album is accompanied by three singles: *cardigan*, *exile* and *betty*. With *cardigan* and *folklore*, she becomes the first artist to have a number-one single and a number-one album on the American charts at the same time. The album also received the Grammy Award for Album of the Year in 2020, making Taylor Swift the only female artist to receive the distinction three times. A few weeks later, she won Artist of the Year at the 2020 American Music Awards for the third year running.

November 25 sees the release of the documentary *Folklore: the long pond studio sessions (en)* on Disney+, in which Taylor Swift performs the folklore songs acoustically at the Long Pond studios and explains each song with Aaron Dessner and Jack Antonoff.

Sixteen hours before its streaming release on December 11, Swift announces the release of her ninth studio album, *evermore*, considered the "little sister" of *folklore*, released a few months earlier. With *willow* and *evermore*, she becomes for the second time the first artist to have both a single and an album number one in the US charts at the same time.

Fearless (Taylor's Version) (April 2021)

In the wake of losing the rights to her first six albums after her former label Big Machine Records was bought out by Scooter Braun, who then sold the catalog to Shamrock Holdings, an investment fund, Taylor Swift announces the release of the re-recorded version of her 2008 single *Love Story*, titled *Love Story (Taylor's Version)* on February 12, 2021, as well as the release of the re-recorded version of *Fearless* (2008), titled *Fearless (Taylor's Version)* for April 9, 2021.

The singer chose to preview her track *Love Story* from her 2008 album *Fearless. The* singer's first big hit, number one in Canada and Australia, and number four on the *Billboard* Hot 100, the song sold over 18 million copies, making it one of the biggest hits of 2008. The re-recorded song debuts at #1 on the *Billboard* Hot 100 Country Songs chart, almost 13 years after its release, and at #11[e] on the U.S. chart across all genres.

Fearless (Taylor's Version) was preceded by three singles, all of which reached the top 10 of the *Billboard* Hot Country Songs chart: *Love Story* reached number one, *You All Over Me reached number* six, followed by *Mr. Perfectly Fine* reaching number two. It reached #1 in Australia, Canada, Ireland, New Zealand, Scotland, the UK and the US, becoming the first re-recorded album ever to top the *Billboard* 200 chart and marking Taylor Swift's ninth #1 album.

Red (Taylor's Version) (November 2021)

On June 18, 2021, Taylor Swift published on social networks the cover of the forthcoming re-recording, *Red (Taylor's Version)*, to be released on November 12, 2021, featuring 30 songs, including 8 "*From the Vault*" and a 10-minute version of a song from the album: *All Too Well* . The album's tracklist was unveiled on August 6, 2021. On its release, *Red (Taylor's Version)* breaks listening records on Spotify, becoming the most listened-to album in one day in the platform's history for a female artist. Taylor Swift also became the most listened-to artist in a single day, with 122.9 million streams.

Despite the lack of radio promotion, *All Too Well (Taylor's Version)* reaches #1 on the *Billboard* Hot 100 a week after its release, becoming her eighth #1 hit in the United States. This set a new record for Taylor Swift, as *All Too*

Well became the longest song in chart history to reach number one (10 minutes and 13 seconds).

Both albums rank among the top 25 best-selling albums of the year. The same year, she appears on four singles in collaboration with other artists: *Renegade (en)* and *Birch* by Big Red Machine (en), a remix of the song *Gasoline (en)* by the band Haim and *The Joker and the Queen (en)* by Ed Sheeran. She also releases *Carolina,* used as the soundtrack to the film *Là où chantent les écrevisses*.

Back to pop with *Midnights* and launch of The Eras Tour (2022-)

During her acceptance speech at the MTV Video Music Awards 2022, Taylor Swift announced the release of her tenth studio album *Midnights on* October 21. The album marks her return to a more pop sound, and breaks records worldwide. The album and its first single *Anti-Hero* become the most listened-to album and song on the Spotify platform in one day, with 185 and 17.4 million streams respectively . She became the first artist to occupy every position in the Billboard Hot 100 top 10, with *Anti-Hero at number* one, *Lavender Haze* at number two and *Snow on the beach (ft Lana del Rey)* at number four. To promote her new album as well as *Lover* (2019), *Folklore* and *Evermore* (2020), she announces a world tour for 2023 called *The Eras Tour*, during which she sings songs from all her many albums or "eras". A film version is scheduled for cinema release on October 13, 2023.

To celebrate her world tour (The Eras Tour), Taylor Swift announces the release of four songs: *Eyes Open (Taylor's Version)*, *Safe & Sound (feat Joy Williams and john boy) (Taylor's Version)*,*If This Was A Movie (Taylor's Version)* and *All Of The Girls You Loved Before*.

Speak Now (Taylor's Version)

In July 2023, she released her third re-recorded album, *Speak Now (Taylor's Version)*, a new version of her 2010 album *Speak Now.* After just 4 days on the market, it becomes the best-selling album of its first week and reaches #1 on the Billboard 200, the first re-recording to achieve this feat.

1989 (Taylor's Version)

Two songs originally featured on the *1989* album have been re-recorded and are available, *Wildest Dreams (Taylor's Version)* since September 17, 2021 and *This Love (Taylor's Version)* since May 6, 2022 . The release of the *1989* re-recording was announced at the last concert of the American leg of her tour in August 2023, and is scheduled for October 27.

Acting career

Swift made her acting debut in 2009, starring in an episode of the forensics TV series *CSI*, in which she played a rebellious teenager. *The New York Times* notes that this role allowed her to be "a little mean and believable." *Rolling Stone* declares that she "did her own thing" and "did a good job with the script", while the *Chicago Tribune* explains that she "acquits herself well." Later in the year, she also presents and performs on *Saturday Night Live*. *Entertainment Weekly* describes her as "*SNL's* best anchor of the season," noting that she "was always up for a challenge, seemed to be having fun and helped the rest of the cast with the punchlines." All the while showing herself to be "admirably flexible in a wide variety of sketch roles."

In 2010, she made her film debut in the romantic comedy *Valentine's Day, playing* the ditzy girlfriend of the most popular boy in high school. *The Los Angeles Times* declares that "her performance had both serious and comic potential", while the *San Francisco Chronicle* finds her very funny. *Time* notes that Swift played her role "in a very charming way"; *The Boston Globe* describes her as "adorably dumb"; salon.com says she was "one of the other actors who wasn't lost in the movie. Her look and eyes were a little reminiscent of Marilyn Monroe and

Lucille Ball." However, *Variety* finds her "undirected... She needs to find an experienced director in order to tamp her down and channel her abundant energy."

In 2012, she lends her voice to the character of Audrey in the animated film *The Lorax*. In 2013, she takes part in the series *New Girl* as Elaine. In 2014, Taylor Swift played the role of Rosemary in Phillip Noyce's film *The Giver.* She played the role of Bombalurina in Tom Hooper's film adaptation of Andrew Lloyd Webber's musical *Cats,* released in late 2019, and also performed one of the songs on the soundtrack, entitled *Beautiful Ghosts*.

In 2021, Swift was announced in the cast of the film *Amsterdam* directed by David O. Russell. The film will be released in the U.S. on October 7, 2022.

Artistic talent

Influences

One of her earliest musical memories is of listening to her maternal grandmother, Marjorie Finlay (née Moehlenkamp), sing. In her youth, Marjorie Finlay was a recording star in Puerto Rico and performed in operas in Singapore: "She was in *The Bartered Bride*, *The Barber of Seville* and musicals like *West Side Story*". As a child, Swift was very fond of songs from Disney films: "My parents noticed that, whenever I ran out of words, I would make up for it with my own words."' . Later on, her parents introduced her to artists such as James Vernon Swift, Simon and Garfunkel, Def Leppard and Smokey Robinson'' . Swift says she owes her confidence to her mother, who as a child helped her prepare her class presentations: "The night before, we'd stay up all night, trying out new things.". She also attributes her "fascination with writing and storytelling" to her mother: "When I was little, she would indulge my imagination and tell me stories." Swift enjoyed reading and writing poetry, and was drawn to the work of Shel Silverstein and Theodor Seuss Geisel. She was interested in "all writing from a child's point of view" and cites Harper Lee's *Don't Shoot the Mockingbird* as one of her favorite books.

Swift's interest in country music began with Shania Twain, Faith Hill and Dixie Chicks. These three artists really let her "decide what she wanted" and she became "enamored with the sound and storytelling" of country . She cites Shania Twain as her biggest influence: "She was so strong, so independent and she wrote all her songs alone." As an artist, Swift says she can only "aspire to be like her" and in 2009; she cites the album *Come on Over* as her favorite . She was able to meet Shania Twain and, later, Shania Twain said she wanted to write a song with Swift. Faith Hill was Swift's role model, and Swift tried to copy her "in what she said, did and wore." She admired Faith for "bringing country music to a wider audience, and her grace in the spotlight." Since her debut, Faith has become a "warm, welcoming presence" in Swift's life. Faith and her husband Tim McGraw once lent her their home in Los Angeles for the duration of her stay there. She then began to take an interest in famous country artists such as Patsy Cline, Loretta Lynn, Tammy Wynette and Dolly Parton. Swift declares that Dolly Parton is "a great example for all female artists... There's so much about Dolly Parton that other female artists should learn from." She also admires Miranda Lambert, Dwight Yoakam, George Strait, Garth Brooks, Kenny Chesney, Reba McEntire, Alan Jackson, Martina McBride, LeAnn Rimes, Tim McGraw and Brad Paisley, Ryan Adams, Patty Griffin, Lori McKenna, and Bon Iver.

Apart from country music, Swift has also been influenced by pop artists such as Hanson, Madonna and Britney Spears; indeed, she still has an "unwavering devotion" to Britney. During her high school years, Swift listened to Dashboard Confessional, Fall Out Boy, Jimmy Eat World, Michelle Branch, Pink, Alanis Morissette, Ashlee Simpson, Kelly Clarkson, Avril Lavigne and Fefe Dobson. She was also a hip-hop fan and listened a lot to Eminem. She describes Stevie Nicks as her main influence: "she inspired me in every way' ." She also loved The Shirelles, Doris Troy and The Beach Boys. She also listened to pop-rock music such as Pat Benatar, Melissa Etheridge, Sarah McLachlan, Sheryl Crow, Shawn Colvin and Linda Ronstadt' . She cites Paul McCartney, Bruce Springsteen, Emmylou Harris and Kris Kristofferson as her career role models: "They took risks, but they stayed the same throughout their careers."" .

Neil Young describes Swift as "an incredible lyricist": "I like listening to her. I like watching her respond to all those attacks. I like the way she defines herself. So I keep an eye on her' ." Kris Kristofferson: "She amazes me. I think it's incredible that someone so young can write such beautiful songs. She has a great career ahead of her' . Dolly Parton is "impressed by her, especially her songwriting... I'm really impressed by her depth. She has the qualities to last a long time." Swift also receives many compliments and congratulations from Alicia Keys, Kelly Clarkson, Lady Gaga and Christopher Owens.

Musical style and themes

Taylor Swift is considered one of the best songwriters of her generation by several publications' . She considers herself first and foremost a lyricist, and that her "voice is just a way of getting these lyrics across". She categorizes her lyrics into three categories: "paroles à la plume", referring to lyrics rooted in archaic poeticism; "paroles au stylo-plume", based on lively, modern plots; and "paroles au stylo à gel scintillant", for lyrics that are lively and frivolous.

The Guardian notes that Swift was "incredibly good at looking at teenage life with a kind of melancholy energy and sepia tone for her first and second albums". *New York Magazine* notes that some singer-songwriters write "about their adolescence... Her closest antecedent is probably Brian Wilson, the real teen author before she came along." They also compare her to Janis Ian. A fairy-tale imagery is presented on the album *Fearless*. For this album, she explores the gap between "fairy tales and the reality of love": "As children, we grow up thinking we're princesses and that a Prince Charming is waiting for us' ." Her third and fourth albums evoke more adult relationships. In addition to love relationships, Swift's songs also deal with parent-child relationships (*The Best*

Day, Ever Grow Up and *Ronan*), friendship (*Fifteen, Breathe* and *22*), detachment (*The Outside, A Place In This World, Tied Together with a Smile* and *Mean*) and professional ambitions (*Change, Long Live* and *The Lucky One*)ʲ . Her defining quality as a songwriter has been described as "a determination to record and hold on to fleeting feelings and impressions, a pre-emptive nostalgia for a present (sometimes even a future) she knows will one day be part of the past." Swift very often incorporates "a phrase thrown into the air that suggests serious, broad things and is poorly integrated into the song, things that reinforce or circumvent the narrative." *The New Yorker* declares that his songs "while not subversive, have a certain elegance.... The sentimental songs are laced with hints of future disillusionment."

Structurally, *Slate* sees in Swift "an ease, a supernatural mastery of pop conventions: very few artists can make bridges the way she does." Swift uses autobiographical details in her songwriting. As a child, she listened to music a lot and felt confused "when I knew something was wrong in an artist's personal life and they didn't address it in their music." *The New York Times* believed that "repairing injustice is what[lle] Swift is all about." In her songs, Swift often addresses "her crushes when she was in high school" and, more recently, her reputed former boyfriends. *Entertainment Weekly* notes that her album *Speak Now* was sometimes "a bit like The *Mole Game*."

59

John Mayer, who inspired Swift for the song *Dear John*,
says the song is a humiliation for him: I think it's kind of a
cheap song. I know he's an international mega star, and
I'm not trying to torpedo anybody, but I think it's beneath
his talent to gloat and say, "Wait till he gets that!" *New
York Magazine* thought that, the media's decision to keep
an eye on her decision to use personal details, "is just
sexist, in that it wasn't requested by her male partners."
The performer herself states that her songs are not based
on facts and are often based on observations. Apart from
the lyrics, which are taken as clues, Swift doesn't try to
talk specifically about the subjects covered in her songs
"because they're real people. You try to give a glimpse of
where you're coming from, as a songwriter, but without
throwing anyone under the bus."

Privacy policy

According to *Forbes* magazine, Taylor Swift raked in $18 million in 2009, $45 million in 2010, $45 million in 2011, $64 million in 2012, $55 million in 2013, and $64 million in 2014. Between June 2014 and May 2015, her earnings reached $80 million. Taylor Swift doubled her earnings between June 2015 and May 2016, taking in $170 million. Between June 2016 and May 2017, she earns $44 million. Between June 2017 and May 2018, her income rises to $80 million, thanks in particular to the release of her album *Reputation*, which sold 4.5 million copies, including 2 million in the United States. She earns $185 million between June 2018 and May 2019, mainly from her Reputation Stadium Tour, the second most lucrative female tour of all time. She then becomes the highest-paid personality according to the Forbes ranking, ahead of Kylie Jenner. Her personal fortune is estimated by *Forbes at* $400 million in 2019.

In 2015 and 2019, Andrea Swift, the singer's mom, was diagnosed with breast cancer. Then in January 2020, Taylor Swift revealed that her mom had been diagnosed with a brain tumor while undergoing treatment for breast cancer recurrence. For her album *Lover*, Taylor Swift writes the song *Soon You'll Get Better*, in which she evokes the health problems both her parents have encountered in recent years.

In August 2017, a lawsuit was filed against an ex-DJ whom she accused of sexual assault. She wins her case on August 14, and receives a symbolic $1 in compensation.

In 2020, Taylor Swift revealed in her documentary *Miss Americana* that she had been battling eating disorders for many years.

In May 2022, she received an honorary Doctor of Fine Arts degree from New York University, and declaimed an encouraging speech to NYU's new graduates.

Sentimental life

From July to October 2008, Taylor Swift was in a relationship with Joe Jonas, member of the Jonas Brothers. At the time, their break-up caused quite a stir, with the 18-year-old singer revealing on the Ellen DeGeneres show that Joe Jonas left her over the phone in 27 seconds.

In the summer of 2009, Taylor Swift met Taylor Lautner on the set of the film *Valentine's Day*; they dated from September to December 2009'.

In December 2009, she began a relationship with John Mayer, whom she had met a year earlier at the Met Gala. They separated in March 2010'.

In October 2010, she began dating actor Jake Gyllenhaal, nine years her senior. Until March 2011, they separated and reconciled several times' . The break-up left a lasting impression on the 21-year-old singer, who went on to write the song *All Too Well*, which became a hit with fans' .

In spring 2012, she had a brief romance with Harry Styles, member of One Direction. From July to September 2012, she dated Conor Kennedy, a member of the Kennedy family' . In September 2012, she got back together with Harry Styles until January 2013' . Shortly after their breakup, Taylor Swift briefly flirted with British singer Tom Odell.

On February 25, 2015, Taylor Swift met British DJ Calvin Harris at the Elle Style Awards - whom she began dating on March 6, 2015. Together, they compose the famous song *This Is What You Came For*, which they then give to Rihanna. The couple split in May 2016 on bad terms. In June 2015, they had topped the list of the highest-paid celebrity couple with an estimated fortune of around $146 million, according to *Forbes* magazine.

On May 2, 2016, Taylor Swift met British actor Tom Hiddleston at the Met Gala, with whom she became a couple a month later, shortly after her breakup with Calvin Harris. They parted amicably in early September 2016.

From September 28, 2016, Taylor Swift shared her life with British actor Joe Alwyn′ . The couple separated in early April 2023 after more than six years of relationship.

In May 2023, the press revealed that Taylor Swift was dating Matty Healy, a member of British rock band The 1975″ . However, on June 5, 2023, TMZ announced that the couple had separated.

Public image

Swift is described as "America's sweetheart" as well as a "role model." She earns a high Q Score (a measure of celebrity awareness and appeal) and good ratings from the David-Brown Index, reflecting high levels of public awareness (90%) and popularity (80%) in the U.S. alone. Swift takes this "responsibility" very seriously, and is aware of the influence she has on her younger fans. A *Rolling Stone* journalist who profiled Swift remarked on her good manners: "If that's a false image Taylor is giving then it must be tattooed on her face because she never falls down." In 2012, *Rolling Stone* notes that Swift presents "an ease with discounts... it's not hard to imagine her running for office, one day," while *The Hollywood Reporter* spoke of her as "The best person since Bill Clinton." She is said to be "the kind of passionate, intensely ambitious person who thrives regardless of her profession." In 2012, *Vogue* magazine described Swift as "smart, funny and sometimes downright bawdy." *Grantland.com* describes her as "nerdy" and "overtly neurotic in a way you'd never see a blonde country princess like Faith Hill or even Carrie Underwood. She's more like Diane Keaton from *Annie Hall*; too graceful and wanting to please but full of nervous, buoyant energy that never stops."

In the early years of her career, Swift's personal style of dress was summer dresses with a pair of Santiag' . This style of dress is still adopted by her young fans who attend her concerts' . At formal events, Swift is known for her "shiny, beaded" dresses. Her naturally curly hair is often reproduced by her fans, and Swift remarks: "I remember when I was a teenager, I used to straighten my hair because I wanted to be like everyone else, and now the fact that everyone else is curling their hair like me.... It's just too much fun." Swift loves retro style and is said to have "30s style; red lipstick, thick mascara' ." In 2011, she was named "American Fashion Icon" by *Vogue*. She cites Françoise Hardy, Jane Birkin, Brigitte Bardot and Audrey Hepburn as her fashion inspirations.

Several comments are made by the media regarding Swift's reactions at awards ceremonies. In 2011, *The Hollywood Reporter* noted that Swift "seemed constantly shocked and amazed every time she won an award." Kristen Wiig parodies Swift's facial expressions during a sketch on *Saturday Night Live* in 2012. Swift later claimed to have seen the sketch: "I laughed all the way through the sketch and then I realized, as I watched the episode, I was making the same expressions as her." That same year, *Academy of Country Music Awards* presenter Blake Shelton joked that Swift should release a perfume called "I can't believe I smell this good". In an interview with *Nightline* in October 2012, Swift laughingly declares that "people make fun of me a lot." Although, at times, she tries to sound blasé: "It's hard when you get excited about something. It's like when you win an award; isn't it something crazy? [...] How can you stand there and say: Oh, another Grammy. I guess I have to get up and get it now".

In August 2022, she was ranked as the most polluting celebrity due to the excessive use of her private jet, and received much criticism on social networks.

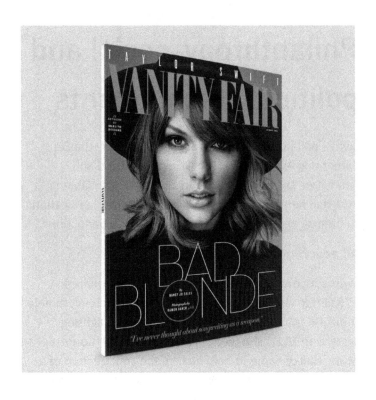

Philanthropy, social and political commitments

Swift's philanthropic efforts are recognized by the Do Something Awards (en), The Giving Back Fund and Tennessee Disaster Services. In 2012, Michelle Obama awarded her the "Best Helper" award for her "dedication to others" and for "inspiring others through her actions."

Art education

Swift supports arts education. In 2010, she donated $75,000 to Nashville's Hendersonville High School, to help refurbish the school's auditorium sound and lighting system. In 2012, she pledges $4 million to the Country Music Hall of Fame to help finance the construction of a new education center in Nashville. Scheduled to open in 2014, the new education center will facilitate new programs and workshops for teens as well as seniors. The building will also feature three classrooms, exhibition space and host interactive activities; a music room and space to make concert posters and other art projects. Museum officials decide to name the center The Taylor Swift Education Center, and the singer participates in an advisory capacity. That same year, Swift partnered with textbook rental company Chegg to donate $60,000 to the music departments of six American colleges' .

Children's literacy

Swift promotes children's literacy. In 2009, she donated $250,000 to a number of schools across the country, some of which she had already visited and others with which she had previously partnered. The money was used to buy books, fund teaching programs and help pay teachers' salaries. In 2010, she took part in the webcast, *Read Now! with Taylor Swift*, broadcast exclusively to US schools to celebrate Scholastic Corporation's Read Every Day campaign. In 2011, Swift donated 6,000 Scholastic books to the Reading Public Library (Pennsylvania), and, in 2012, she donated 14,000 books to the Nashville Public Library (Tennessee). Most of the books were put into circulation, and the rest were donated to children from low-income families, nursery schools and day-care centers. In 2012, she co-chaired the Read Across America campaign, organized by the National Education Association, and registered a PSA (Public Service Announcement) to encourage children to read' . That same year, she promoted the "power of reading" in a second webcast. In 2013, through the Reach Out and Read initiative, she donates 2,000 books to Scholastic at Reading Hospital Child Health Center.

Natural disasters

Throughout her career, Swift has repeatedly helped victims of natural disasters. In 2008, she donated the proceeds from her Country Music Festival product sales to disaster relief funds. Later that year, she donated $100,000 to the American Red Cross to help victims of the 2008 Iowa floods. In 2009, she supports the Victorian wildfires of 2009 by joining the Sound Relief concert line-up in Sydney and making the largest contribution. In January 2010, she took part in the Telethon organized by George Clooney for the 2010 earthquake in Haiti, playing and answering calls for donations. She also recorded a song for the *Hope for Haiti Now* album. Following the Nashville floods in May 2010, Swift donated $500,000 at a telethon. Later that year, she donated $100,000 to help fund the rebuilding of a playground in Hendersonville.

In 2011, she used the final dress rehearsal of a North American concert on her Speak Now World Tour as a benefit concert for the victims of the tornado outbreak in the USA from April 25 to 28, 2011. She also donates $250,000 to Nick Saban's Nick's Kids charity, the coach of Alabama's Crimson Tide soccer team. In 2012, Swift supports Architecture for Humanity - which helped restore the hall where telethons are held - for the damage caused by Hurricane Sandy.

Commitment to fighting homophobia

Swift opposes discrimination against the LGBT community. Following the murder of Larry King in February 2008, Swift joined the Gay, Lesbian and Straight Education Network, an organization that fights hate crimes. A year after Larry King's murder, Swift tells *Seventeen* magazine that her parents taught her "never to judge someone based on who they love, their skin color or their religion." In 2011, the video for the single *Mean* also denounced homophobia within high schools; later, the clip was nominated for an MTV VMA in the "Social Commitment" category" . *The New York Times* believes she is part of "the new wave of young women who are offering songs for a generation of gay fans to reconnect with their identity in a time of turbulence and confused cultural messages." She also defends the rights of the LGBTQ+ community in her single You Need To Calm Down.

Charitable organizations

Swift is involved in numerous charities for sick children. In 2008, she donated a pink Chevrolet van to the Victory Junction Gang Camp; the van is used to transport sick children from the airport to the camp. In 2009, after singing at the *Children in Need* Telethon, she donated $20,000. In 2011, as the Academy of Country Music's Artist of the Year, she donated $25,000 to St. Jude Children's Research Hospital in Tennessee. In 2012, she took part in the telethon organized by the charity *Stand Up to Cancer*, performing *Ronan*, a song she wrote in memory of a 4-year-old boy who died of neuroblastoma. The song was made available as a paid digital download, with proceeds subsequently donated to neuroblastoma charities. At the same time, she met many sick children through the Make-A-Wish association' . She also makes private visits to hospitals such as St. Jude Children's Research Hospital, Walter Reed Army Medical Center and Ronald McDonald House" .

Other charitable activities

Swift encourages young people to volunteer in their local communities and is part of Global Youth Service Day. She also promotes the @15 Fund, a social change platform that gives young people the opportunity to lead the philanthropic company. In 2007, she launched a campaign to protect children from sexual "predators", in partnership with the Tennessee Association of Chiefs of Police. That same year, she promoted an Allstate campaign to ensure safe driving for teenagers. In 2010, she posed for the *Got Milk?* campaign. She also sings in numerous charity concerts" .

Political commitment

In the 2018 midterm elections, she calls on young people to register to vote and vote for Democrats. In particular, she supports Democrat Phil Bredesen, who was running for governor of Tennessee against Republican Marsha Blackburn. The press rejoiced at the sharp increase in the number of registered voters (over 13,000 between June 7 and 10 in Tennessee alone, and 166,000 nationwide). Nevertheless, while Phil Bredesen dominated the polls until September, Marsha Blackburn won the election in November by almost 11 points over her opponent .

Discography

Tours

- 2009-2010: *Fearless Tour*

- 2011-2012: *Speak Now World Tour*

- 2013-2014: *Red Tour*

- 2015: *The 1989 World Tour*

- 2018: *Reputation Stadium Tour*

- 2023-2024: *The Eras Tour*

Filmography

- 2009: *CSI* (TV series) - Season 9, episode 16: Haley Jones

- 2009: *Saturday Night Live*: Own role (presenter)

- 2013: *New Girl* (TV series) - Season 2, episode 25: Elaine

- 2019 : *The Voice : La Plus Belle Voix* : Elle-même (Quarter Finals : Sing with the Talents)

Cinema

- 2008: *Jonas Brothers: The Concert Event* by Bruce Hendricks: Own role (cameo)

- 2009: *Hannah Montana, the film* by Peter Chelsom: Own role (cameo)

- 2010: *Valentine's Day* by Garry Marshall: Felicia

- 2012: *Le Lorax* by Chris Renaud: Audrey (voice)

- 2014: *The Giver* by Phillip Noyce: Rosemary

- 2019: *Cats* by Tom Hooper: Bombalurina

- 2020: *Miss Americana* by Lana Wilson: Herself

- 2022 : *Amsterdam* by David O. Russell: Liz Meekins

Other books by United Library

https://campsite.bio/unitedlibrary